GLASGOW–TOKYO LINE

ALSO BY JAMES MCGONIGAL

Driven Home (Mariscat Press, 1998)
Passage/An Pasaíste (Mariscat Press, 2004)
Cloud Pibroch (Mariscat Press, 2010)
The Camphill Wren (Red Squirrel Press, 2016)
Turning Over in a Strange Bed (Mariscat Press, 2017)
In Good Time (Red Squirrel Press, 2020)
Envy the Seasons (Tapsalteerie Press, 2022; with Iain Maloney & Hamish Whyte)
Life Sentences (Red Squirrel Press, 2023)

CRITICAL AND EDITED WORKS

Sons of Ezra: British Poets and Ezra Pound (with Michael Alexander, 1995)
Beyond the Last Dragon: A Life of Edwin Morgan (2010, 2012)
Edwin Morgan: *The Midnight Letterbox. Selected Correspondence* (with John Coyle, 2015)

ALSO BY JOHN PAZDZIORA

Leaving Concord: Poems (ITIA, 2014)
Smout and the Lighthouse (Albert Whitman, 2023; with Jane Yolen)

LIBRETTI AND SUNG TEXTS (MUSIC BY ERIC M. PAZDZIORA)

Dr. Milliner's Marvellous Musical Flying Machine (2012)
Canticles for the Holy Innocents (2015)
Nativity of the Isles (2018)
House of Winter: Opera in One Act (2018)
Nocturne, Midsummer (2021)

Glasgow–Tokyo Line

An East–West Hyakuin

James McGonigal & John Pazdziora

ISOBAR
PRESS

Published in 2026 by

Isobar Press
Sakura 2-21-23-202, Setagaya-ku,
Tokyo 156-0053, Japan

https://isobarpress.com

ISBN 978-4-907359-54-6

COVER IMAGE

KATSUSHIKA HOKUSAI, *Viewing the Sunset over Ryōgoku Bridge from the Onmaya Embankment* (Onmayagashi yori Ryōgokubashi sekiyō o miru), from the series *Thirty-six Views of Mount Fuji* (Fugaku sanjūrokkei), 1830–31. Metropolitan Museum of Art, New York; Henry L. Phillips Collection, Bequest of Henry L. Phillips, 1939. www.metmuseum.org

To all our children

GLASGOW–TOKYO LINE

Two of a similar spirit have met;

who can distinguish host from guest?

序

あおうめや *ao ume ya*

Three ducklings chase their shadows
down the drainage ditch.

Our washed-away bridge rebuilt.
Plump berries wait: wild, sweet.

Window boxes sprout
green peppers in summer grass.
I didna plant that.

Stretching for plums, my fingers
greet a snail. Good day, neighbour.

Thunderheads this evening.
Five sunflowers sway above
hedge branches uncut.

Unkempt leaves. Twa laddies
run past, loose frae school.

Tractors growl down
eggplant rows across the street
せみの声 *semi no koe*

Fledglings long flown. Listen:
bees building in the nestbox.

一

Can fresh leaves foretell
the snick-snap of garden shears
on October days?

In time, pencil marks crumble.
My ballpoint ticks on the page.

Eftir lang days, gane.
The dochter pegs white sheets oot
hoo her mither tocht.

Crisp white crease, a mountain fold,
soon cranes circle the garden.

Cucumber horses
and aubergine cows! Stick legs
trot across gravestones.

Late again. Umeboshi
crinkle in Obon heat.

Children, please carry
a soup bowl and glass of wine
to this spot. And drink.

I hae few halie corners.
A kirkyaird, a cradle. Ach.

Place gifts close enough
for their old hands to grip –
rain washes the tomb.

Storms gaither, blotching the moon:
summer is the time for ghosts.

Why redd up the hoose
whan naebody veesits, bar
the deid? Guid reason!

Already autumn has scorched
and bent waterside grasses.

Laden with nectar
a bee dislodges petals,
lifting off late blooms.

Vermillion dragonflies
flicker among dry reeds.

二

Twa dreams yestreen.
A blackie wheechs awa then turns
grey as this smirr –

Fog-blotched fretful octopus,
Old Mother Fuji brooding.

Early mists adrift.
Has every tree just taken
one step closer – ?

Trust the oak and the great beech,
but shun both ash and alder.

This calligraphy
of memory – her face
comes and goes like that.

Frost leaves ghosts on the window.
Weave a circle round them thrice.

In October grass
a manuscript of mushrooms,
ancient as Gaelic.

Green tracks in rain-bright pasture.
A handprint fogs the cover.

The hazier line
of fells in autumn weather.
My heart in free-fall.

After a steep mountain run,
why are my sleeves still wet – ?

Those far hills, blue-grey.
Old folk thinking: which of us
will see winter out?

A dog sleeps at the turnstile,
waiting for his master's scent.

Memories of blossom
scattering down our street.
White slow thinning moon.

Turn awa. Shut the windae.
I cannae bear the licht –

三

First day of winter.
The sky weaves a herringbone
tweed of dun and grey.

Not too cold for cycling yet,
I say. At dusk, frost settles.

Boughs bent with red haws
over waterfall bubbles.
My old eyes lose count.

In my closet, six glass jars
glowing salt on 梅 skin. *ume*

Put on winter clothes –
garments smelling of woodsmoke,
grass, lichen, and rain.

This carpet stinks o whisky.
Wheesht, Jimmy, pour anither!

The forecast says snow
from the east. Eyes at windows
say goodbye to green.

Yellow gingko avenue,
gold leaves, rancid butter reek.

Thorny bush burning
with berries. Pigeons gorging
till their beaks turn gold.

A giant hornet creepit
for warmth on a lassie's shin.

Roused by cold, the pond
shivers, then glares. My right eye
appraises the day.

Moonlight runs white through ice clouds,
pigeon-spatter on the path.

Tea from the green cup.
Morning mist slowly rising
touches my forehead.

Red bags of coffee stacked high.
Choirboys heralding Christmas.

四

Smoke tastes of whisky.
Brittle branches we pile up
to conquer the cold.

Red wine at the kotatsu.
We pluck mikan-peel bouquets.

Stirring my porridge
and composing this haiku.
Sunrise on the fells.

Dark long before teatime, now.
Will I type or write by hand?

Garden library.
Bibliography of frost.
Leaf sparkle studies.

About the author: 'Here lies
the green as oft as the white.'

Snowflakes on heather.
Dawn shakes my shoulder. I grunt:
Just go back to sleep.

Gesticulating skyward,
tattie-bogie nicks the mune.

Meenits and years built
this hoose. A dreich sky tims oot
rain frae rustit bowls.

My mind’s wanderin’ the noo.
I maun mend the birch fence.

High on the glenside
I’m listening for poetry:
grey-horned, soft-eared. Wheesht.

‘Sometimes,’ she says, ‘there’s an owl,
and sometimes, aye, there isnae.’

Her grave happt wi snaw.
Whase buit-prents are thae, trauchlin
up till't, syne awa.

Light the candles, remember
laughter we never heard –

五

Laddies ran dyke-taps,
airms wide. Airms wide noo, here's me
shauchlin icy lanes.

The park fence verges the tracks.
Children cheer the passing trains.

I remember north:
thistles glowering through barbed wire
by the drainage ditch.

Nets of fairy lights glamour
the train station roundabout.

Last leaves on the tree
clinging to their ancestry.
Noble earth, fine rain.

Hot sake, mikan pips,
snug chatter, tending to sleep.

Crumbs for the robin.
Winter breath comes ghosting from
an old man's nostrils.

We munch on gingerbread men
and watch Scrooge flit through time.

Solve death's equation.
The brightest of my old school
pals are struggling now.

Unbearable, this tortoise
shuffle towards Christmas morning.

Fox-paw tracks on snow.
My hunter eyes follow his
through last night's moonset.

What's that rumpus at sunrise?
Children tear open the day.

Snow's on the far woods.
Look, hidden clearings sparkle
in constellations.

Hazy as a fading cloud,
the tree bends. New plum blossom.

六

White breath of cattle.
Hay strands are locked in mud
round the heck today.

Wind kicks dust round the playground,
crusting our baseball with grit.

Homeless and begging.
One outstretched glove, blown over
our wall by the gale.

Dozing at my kotatsu,
I hear rain in the far north.

Down in black and white.
Fresh earth on molehills. Agile
snowdrop fingertips.

Spring thaw hasnae fired the page.
My pen's aye smoorit wi cauld.

I stacked those planks straight.
The forearms of frost and wind
and rain have warped them.

Small shoes crowd the genkan,
claggy with yellow spring mud.

The manifold shades
of blossom escape us. Plum,
apple, cherry. Moon.

An old man waters young trees.
A golden carp slips the net.

Still half-asleep. Heads
up. Shoulders back. Crocuses
marshal on parade.

桜 brush the streetlamp, *sakura*
ice clouds blotting the stars.

Spring's bright first greens, look.
Moss on north-facing branches.
Old folks' wellingtons.

Gently, oor guid auld neibour
draps oor ba' back owre the fence.

急

Sitting with March frost,
what a night of stars unfolds
in my grey curtain.

Dock crane at dawn, hoisting up
boxed cargo through river mist.

Inkstone dry, my brush
blotches lines in the sutra:
天上だ *ten jō da*

Feel my muscles, the earth boasts,
a kid amazed at flesh, bones.

Seven ducklings now.
Water hisses in dry grass
down the spillway –

Pavement pigeons shuffle, spooked
by a runner's fleet shadow.

梅干し heaped *umeboshi*
in salt-crusted mason jars.
Dandelion wine.

Small hands raising empty cups.
Fill them up over the brim.

NOTES

NOTES

A *hyakuin* is the hundred-stanza version of a *renga*, a long-form, collaborative Japanese poem. Today, renga is best known in Western cultures through its descendant, the 17-syllable *haiku*, though the haiku's reputation for a rather lonely, delicate lyricism belies the social and even satirical energies it can express within Japanese culture. That social side is often revealed in the renga form.

A renga consists of alternating 17- and 14-syllable stanzas, the first following a pattern of 5/7/5 syllables and the second of 7/7; these combine like the octave and sestet of a sonnet to form the 31 syllables of a classical *tanka*. The renga makes the pattern collaborative, with two or more poets linking stanzas together in a sort of call and response, weaving their voices into a series which gains coherence through their personal and artistic sympathy. Each new stanza is meant to reflect on the insights of the preceding one, but in a glancing way. Catching the subtle interconnections being made is part of the form's pleasure.

The renga emerged in the twelfth century and reached maturity in the fifteenth, with the works of renga master Sōgi (1421–1502) and his students. At the height of its fashion, a hyakuin renga – or even longer forms – could be composed by an entire roomful of poets during a long, sometimes boozy afternoon. These renga writing sessions often took a playful, competitive tone, with the poets vying to outdo each other with elegant allusions to classical poetry and clever use of established symbols – moon, plum blossoms, autumn rain, frogs singing.

The hyakuin follows a seasonal structure of 100 stanzas, arranged in the threefold structure of *jo-ha-kyū* (序破急). The opening movement *jo* introduces the different voices of the renga, presenting the major themes. For this section, John Pazdziora has written the 5/7/5 stanzas, taking the role of the host; James McGonigal replies in the 7/7 stanzas to the host's greeting, traditionally the voice of the renga master and elder poet. The following movement, the *ha*, develops the themes through six equal sections. Unusually, we have reversed the order of voices in the *ha*, with James McGonigal writing the 5/7/5 stanzas and John Pazdziora replying with the 7/7. The final section is the rapid movement, or *presto*, of the *kyū*, in which the threads of the *ha* weave together in the conclusion. Here, mirroring the *jo*, John Pazdziora once again writes the 5/7/5 stanzas, giving James McGonigal the final word(s) in the 7/7s.

Students of renga, East and West, have cultivated elaborate schemata for the correct ordering of the seasons and placement of seasonal vocabulary. We have not attempted to strictly reproduce any particular system of renga, though sharp-eyed readers will find moons and blossoms in each section, along with echoes of the love stanza. In general, however, we have sought the simpler gate of Bashō (1644–1694), whose radical approach to the renga of his day led to the creation of haiku and who taught a system of thirteen different kinds of link between stanzas. While examples of many of Bashō's links can be found in these pages, our renga has drawn its greatest inspiration from 'the link by scent' (*nioi-zuke*, 匂付), in which, to use the words of Haruo Shirane, 'the added verse is joined to the previous verse by shared connotations, carrying the atmosphere of its predecessor much as the fragrance of a flower is carried by the wind.' We have also complicated the hyakuin's allusive nature by using both Scottish and Japanese landscapes, while employing the almost-immediacy of email to compose the poem over many months.

Thus, rather than the leisure of a golden afternoon, this East-West hyakuin reflects the stop-go intercultural aspects of contemporary life, combining work interruptions with the domestic normality that sustains us. The languages we use or encounter (American and Scottish English, contemporary and historical Japanese, and more ancient Scots) together with their differing calligraphies and writing implements, are also part of the scene. There are other voices echoed in the poem besides our own. The epigraph *Two of a similar spirit have met…* is from the hermit, poet, and calligrapher Ryōkan (1758–1831), in Kazuaki Tanahashi's soulful translation, and bows to what can be achieved at a distance.

Further notes below are not intended to be exhaustive, but simply to clarify some possibly unfamiliar cultural or linguistic features. As the poems are unnumbered, the notes are too, but they appear in their order within each section.

序 INTRODUCTION

あおうめや *ao ume ya*: roughly, 'Green plums, aye.' あお (青, *ao*) is literally 'blue', the colour of unripeness. It is also the *kigo* (季語, season word) which orients the hyakuin in the time of writing – in this case, early spring. や is the *kireji* or cutting word, formally required in the opening stanza. The meaning is difficult to render into English but functionally similar to the Scots 'aye' or 'och aye' or the Ulster 'so it is'. Further appearances of kigo and kireji in the poem will pass without comment.

didna: did not

laddies, frae: young boys, from

せみの声 *semi no koe*: cicadas' voices, a constant presence in Tokyo through the summer months.

一 SECTION I

hoo her mither tocht: as her mother taught

umeboshi: salted and dried Japanese plums (*Prunus mume*), a small, intensely sour fruit, mildly toxic when raw but celestially fragrant when jammed, dried, vinegared, fermented, or stewed.

Obon: the summer fire festival of Bon, when Japanese families return to their hometowns to sweep the graves and honour their ancestors. Much like All Soul's Day or Día de Muertos, the dead are understood to return for a visit during the festival. There are many thoughtful rituals encouraging them to go away again.

redd up: tidy, clean.

bar the deid: apart from the dead

二 SECTION II

yestreen: last night

A blackie wheechs awa: a blackbird rushes off with a whizzing sound

smirr: fine rain

why are my sleeves still wet?: the long sleeves of the poet's gown grow wet through wiping away tears. The question echoes Ryōkan, who was echoing Bashō, who was himself echoing an image that frequently appears in traditional renga. Bewilderment arises because, Ryōkan says, 'I understand the doctrine of impermanence, so why…?'

licht: light

三 SECTION III

ume skins: see note on *umeboshi* above. As the pickled ume dry in the blazing July sun, the salt seeps through their skins and forms a crumpled white coating.

Wheesht: be quiet, shut up

creepit: having crept

四 SECTION IV

kotatsu: a low table, with a heater affixed underneath and draped with a duvet, the centre of Japanese family life in winter.

mikan: a small, pungently sweet citrus (*Citrus unshiu*), better known in English as satsuma or mandarin orange.

tattie-bogie: scarecrow, particularly in a potato field

A dreich sky tims oot: a dreary sky pours out

maun: must

happt: covered over

buit-prents: boot-prints

trauchlin: tramping, shambling

syne awa: then away again

五 SECTION V

dyke-taps: tops of stone walls

shauchlin: shuffling along

New plum blossom: ume trees blossom at the very first whiff of spring in late January, opening pale flowers with a delicate toughness that endeared them to ancient Chinese poets.

六 SECTION VI

heck: slatted wooden rack for fodder

genkan: a small foyer in Japanese buildings, where people pause to remove their shoes before entering.

桜 *sakura*: cherry blossoms

draps oor ba' back owre: drops our ball back over

急 CONCLUSION

天上だ *ten jō da*: literally, 'the sky is up'. The poet began copying Ryōkan's famous calligraphy 天上大風 (*ten jō dai fu* sky overhead, big wind) but muddled the third character with a wonky downstroke.

ACKNOWLEDGEMENTS

The authors thank Paul Rossiter at Isobar Press for his positive response to their work, and for guiding it so skilfully and generously through production. Several of these haiku previously appeared in an 80th birthday tribute to Sukhema (formerly Larry Butler), an American-born Buddhist poet and teacher long resident in Glasgow. We happily extend deep bows of gratitude from Tokyo to Glasgow.

ABOUT THE AUTHORS

James McGonigal has combined professional writing on children's literacy and school language learning with broader publications in biography, literary modernism and Scottish and Irish literature. Poetry is his main creative interest and his work has won prizes in Scotland, Ireland and the UK. He is Professor Emeritus of English in Education at Glasgow University.

John Pazdziora has written poetry, libretti, and children's books in Scotland, China, and Japan. His academic research focuses on the interplay between literature and religion, especially in children's media. He is associate professor in the Department of English at Aoyama Gakuin University in Tokyo.

www.ingramcontent.com/pod-product-compliance
Ingram Content Group UK Ltd.
Pitfield, Milton Keynes, MK11 3LW, UK
UKHW041133271225
466385UK00001B/12

9 784907 359546